Put Beginning Readers on the Right Track with
ALL ABOARD READING™

The All Aboard Reading series is especially designed for beginning readers. Written by noted authors and illustrated in full color, these are books that children really want to read—books to excite their imagination, expand their interests, make them laugh, and support their feelings. With fiction and nonfiction stories that are high interest and curriculum-related, All Aboard Reading books offer something for every young reader. And with four different reading levels, the All Aboard Reading series lets you choose which books are most appropriate for your children and their growing abilities.

Picture Readers
Picture Readers have super-simple texts, with many nouns appearing as rebus pictures. At the end of each book are 24 flash cards—on one side is a rebus picture; on the other side is the written-out word.

Station Stop 1
Station Stop 1 books are best for children who have just begun to read. Simple words and big type make these early reading experiences more comfortable. Picture clues help children to figure out the words on the page. Lots of repetition throughout the text helps children to predict the next word or phrase—an essential step in developing word recognition.

Station Stop 2
Station Stop 2 books are written specifically for children who are reading with help. Short sentences make it easier for early readers to understand what they are reading. Simple plots and simple dialogue help children with reading comprehension.

Station Stop 3
Station Stop 3 books are perfect for children who are reading alone. With longer text and harder words, these books appeal to children who have mastered basic reading skills. More complex stories captivate children who are ready for more challenging books.

In addition to All Aboard Reading books, look for All Aboard Math Readers™ (fiction stories that teach math concepts children are learning in school); All Aboard Science Readers™ (nonfiction books that explore the most fascinating science topics in age-appropriate language); and All Aboard Poetry Readers™ (funny, rhyming poems for readers of all levels).

All Aboard for happy reading!

For Jane O'Connor—thank you—J.D.
To Alex and Max, the two people who
move my world—L.O.

Special thanks to Professor Michael Rampino of New York University for
fact-checking the book.

Photo credits: 10: Bettmann/CORBIS. 11: U.S. Geological Survey. 19: David Parker/Science
Photo Library/Photo Researchers, Inc. 29: Getty Images Inc./Hulton Archive Photos.

Text copyright © 2004 by Jennifer Dussling. Illustrations copyright © 2004 by Lori Osiecki.
All rights reserved. Published by Grosset & Dunlap, a division of Penguin Young Readers
Group, 345 Hudson Street, New York, New York 10014. ALL ABOARD SCIENCE READER
and GROSSET & DUNLAP are trademarks of Penguin Group (USA) Inc. Printed in the
U.S.A.

Library of Congress Cataloging-in-Publication Data

Dussling, Jennifer.
    Earthquakes / by Jennifer Dussling ; illustrated by Lori Osiecki.
       p. cm. — (All aboard science reader. Station stop 2)
    ISBN 0-448-43203-X (pbk.) — ISBN 0-448-43327-3 (hardcover)
    1. Earthquakes—Juvenile literature. 2. Earthquake prediction—Juvenile literature.
[1. Earthquakes.] I. Osiecki, Lori, ill. II. Title. III. Series.
    QE521.3.D88 2004
    551.22—dc22
                                             2003026930

ISBN 0-448-43203-X (pbk)   10 9 8 7 6 5 4 3 2 1
ISBN 0-448-43327-3 (GB)   10 9 8 7 6 5 4 3 2 1

EARTHQUAKES

By Jennifer Dussling
Illustrated by Lori Osiecki

Grosset & Dunlap • New York

Anchorage, Alaska
March 27, 1964

It was Good Friday,

just two days before Easter.

At first, it seemed

like a normal day.

People were at work.

Kids were home after school.

5

Then the world changed.

An earthquake struck!

The ground shook.

Buildings toppled.

Houses fell into the sea.

Cracks opened
in the earth.
Some were
thirty feet wide.

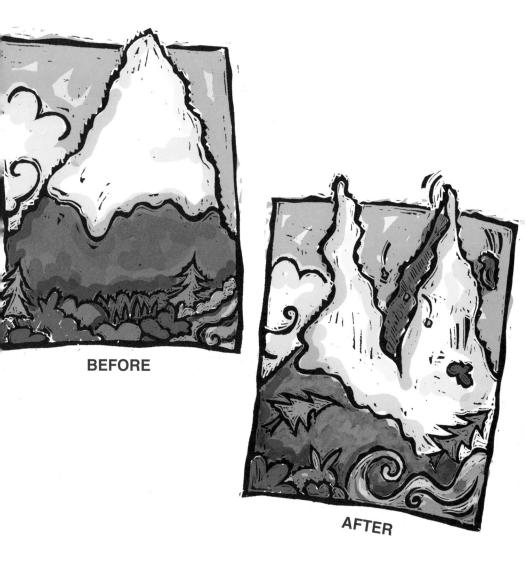

BEFORE

AFTER

A mountain was ripped in two.

One minute, the world was normal.

Four minutes later,

it was tilted and torn

and crooked and broken.

The earthquake in Alaska
was the worst ever recorded
in the United States.
It did a lot of damage.
But what made it happen?
What causes an earthquake?

The earth is like a big ball.

The center is the <u>core</u>.

It is made of metal.

The temperature is hot

enough to melt iron.

The middle layer is

very, very hot rock.

This is the <u>mantle</u>.

On top of the mantle

floats the rocky <u>crust</u>.

The crust is from five

to thirty miles thick.

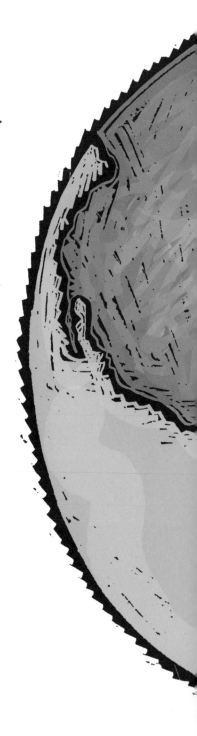

The crust is made of several
huge pieces. Each piece is called
a <u>plate</u>. The plates move very,
very slowly over the mantle.

Sometimes, two plates rub
or scrape against each other.
Pressure builds up in the rock.

Sooner or later, somewhere
in the crust something gives.
Two sides of rock snap free
from each other.
This makes an earthquake.

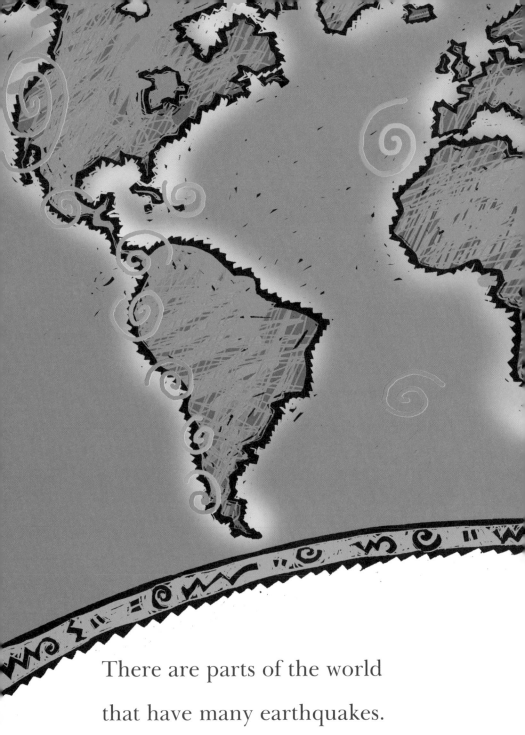

There are parts of the world

that have many earthquakes.

There are parts that never have them.

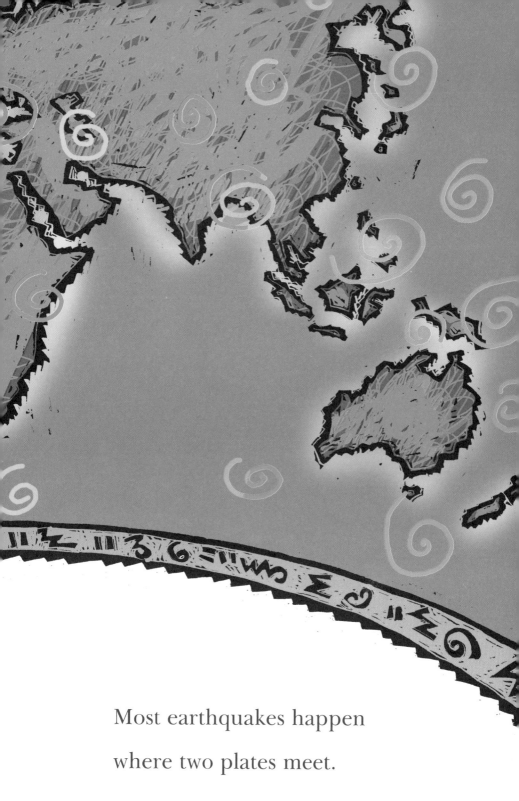

Most earthquakes happen

where two plates meet.

A big crack in the earth

runs through California.

A crack like this is called a <u>fault</u>.

This one is the San Andreas fault.

It goes for hundreds of miles.

A lot of earthquakes happen near a fault. That's because two plates come together here.

People may build a fence.

Then an earthquake hits.

It makes the fence break.

Now there is part of a fence

on either side of the fault!

A machine called a seismograph measures earthquakes.

It records the shaking of the earth on a roll of paper.

The machine rates earthquakes, starting with 1.

You couldn't even feel a 1.

With a level 3, the ground shakes.

What about a 6?

An earthquake with a rating

of 6 or higher,

you wouldn't forget!

There is also another way

to measure earthquakes.

It measures the damage

from an earthquake.

Right where the rock snapped

has the highest rating.

But farther away,

the same earthquake

has a lower rating.

That's because farther away

there is less damage.

When a big quake hits,

there is danger from fires.

In 1906 a big earthquake hit San Francisco.

It was early morning.

People ran out of their homes

in their pajamas.

Buildings shook.

Inside the buildings,

stoves fell over.

Flames leaped out of the stoves.

The wood houses
caught on fire!
Soon almost the whole city
was burning.

The earthquake also broke
many water pipes.

So firemen had a hard
time fighting the fires.
In two days, fire destroyed
five hundred blocks.

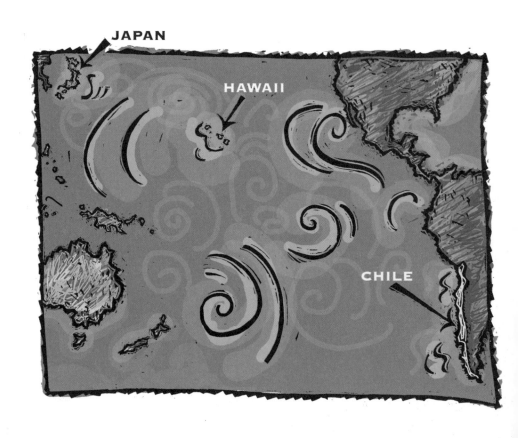

With other quakes,

there is danger of flooding.

On May 22, 1960,

an earthquake hit Chile

in South America.

Chile is on the Pacific coast.

The quake made

big waves in the ocean.

The waves moved
across the ocean.
They got bigger and bigger.
Fifteen hours later,
the waves hit Hawaii.
They were thirty-three feet high!
Scientists knew this
would happen.
They had asked
everyone to stay
away from
the beaches.

But the scientists did not plan

for what happened next.

The waves kept going!

Seven hours later,

they struck Japan.

And no one was ready.

Scientists want to tell

when a quake is coming.

That way, everyone could be ready.

Some scientists think that animals know.

One day in Japan in 1977,

there was a little earthquake.

Was a bigger one on the way?

Scientists watched animals closely.

Many did very strange things.

A rabbit climbed onto a roof.

Rats walked on telephone wires.

Snakes crawled out of the ground

and froze on the snow.

Hours later, a big quake hit.

Right now, there is no sure way

to predict an earthquake.

But builders make stronger buildings.

They use steel, not wood.

In a quake,

these buildings sway instead of fall.

And there are things you
can do in an earthquake.

If you are outside,

stay away from buildings,

tall trees, and power lines.

Go to an open space like a parking lot.

If you are inside,

don't go near

windows or mirrors.

They may shatter.

Hide under a big table

or stand in a doorway.

Never ride an elevator.

Go down a stairway instead.

When the building stops

shaking, get out.